# My First Book of Music Theory

## Carla Louro

Arts2Science

http://www.arts2science.com

ISBN-13: 978-989-8627-31-5

Student's name ----------------------------------------------------

Teacher's name ----------------------------------------------------

Music lesson's schedule ----------------------------------------------------

**Messages from the teacher** →

| | |
|---|---|
| Date: | |
| Message: ---------------------------------------------------- | |
| Date: | |
| Message: ---------------------------------------------------- | |
| Date: | |
| Message: ---------------------------------------------------- | |
| Date: | |
| Message: ---------------------------------------------------- | |
| Date: | |
| Message: ---------------------------------------------------- | |

**Messages from the parents** →

| | |
|---|---|
| Date: | |
| Message: ---------------------------------------------------- | |
| Date: | |
| Message: ---------------------------------------------------- | |
| Date: | |
| Message: ---------------------------------------------------- | |
| Date: | |
| Message: ---------------------------------------------------- | |
| Date: | |
| Message: ---------------------------------------------------- | |

# *About this book*

This book teaches music theory to children. It includes text, exercises and illustrations.

It has three chapters:

1. The music staff and the music notes.

2. Rhythm.

3. Other elements of music: the scales, dynamics, tempo marks, musical instruments and symbols.

The student and the teacher can study different chapters at the same time. This means that the student can learn how to read notes in the treble clef in chapter 1 and learn minims and semibreves in chapter 2.

This book includes note flashcards for the treble clef and the bass clef and several revision exercises.

The mp3 files with the rhythms and melodies from the book can be downloaded at http:// www.arts2science.com. This website has a page dedicated to this book. This page includes internet links with additional information and games about each chapter.

The numbers of the mp3 files appear before each song in the book.

The same page about this book includes a **virtual piano** that the student can play, a virtual game about **the instruments of the orchestra** and a virtual game about the **bass clef**.

# CONTENTS

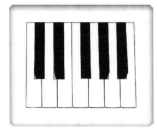

Meet the characters in the book.

The **Penguin** will teach you the musical notes and how to read them in the treble clef and in the bass clef.

The **Ant** will teach you everything about rhythm.

The **Owl** will teach you several musical concepts, terms and abbreviations. You will learn about dynamics, sharps, flats and more.

Now you'll see that learning music theory is fun!

# 1
# The Staff and the Musical Notes

The **Penguin** will teach you the musical notes and how to read them in the treble clef and in the bass clef.

## The Treble Clef

## The Bass Clef

**Chapter One** will teach you how to read the musical notes.

You will learn what is the music staff.

You will learn how to read notes in the treble clef.

You will learn how to read notes in the bass clef.

You have many exercises about the **Musical Notes.**

You will be able to hear the sound of the notes with a **virtual piano.**

—⌇—

*Good Work*

I'm the **penguin** and I will teach you the musical notes.

## The Music Staff

The notes are written on the Music Staff.

The staff has 5 lines and 4 spaces.

5
4
3
2
1

4
3
2
1

**Lines**

**Spaces**

## The Treble Clef

The clef tells you how to read notes on the music staff.

The **treble clef** tells us that the note **G** is on the second line.

**second line**

G

The "Clef" is what is used to assign specific note names to each of the lines and spaces. The "Treble Clef" and the "Bass Clef" are the most common clefs.

The treble clef tells us that the note G is on the second line.

Listen and play the notes at http://www.arts2science.com. Open the application "Virtual Piano", which is located in a folder with the name of this book.

The note names in the Treble Clef are:

| C | D | E | F | G | A | B | C |
|---|---|---|---|---|---|---|---|

**Exercises about the treble clef.**

Write the names of these notes.

Clue

The note G is on the second line.

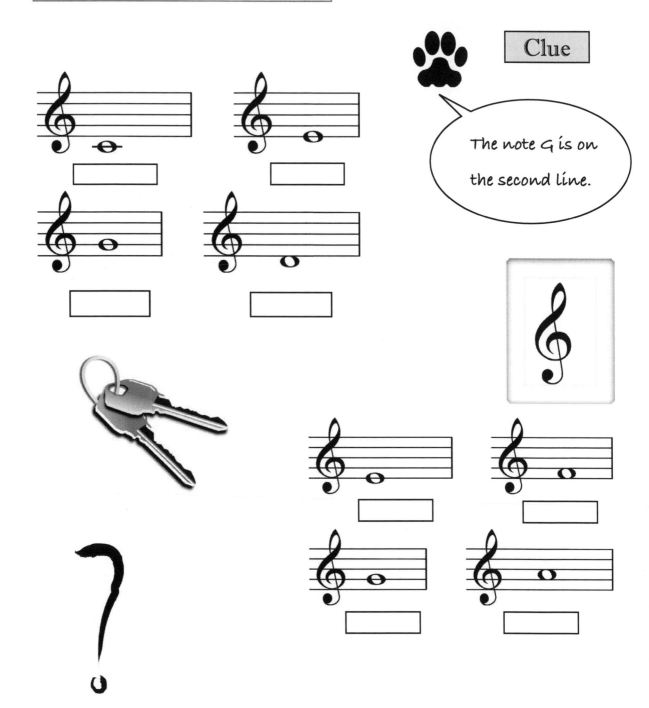

Place each number in the right box.

| Note | Number |
|------|--------|
| B    |        |
| C    |        |

| Note | Number |
|------|--------|
| A    |        |
| G    |        |

1

2

3

4

? Draw the treble clef.

Colour the cat. Use **red** ink.

What's the name of this note?_____

What's the name of this note?_____

You are using colours to start reading the musical notes.

Colour the penguin. Use **blue** ink.

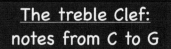

Write the names of the notes. Use colours:
G-**red** and E-**blue**.

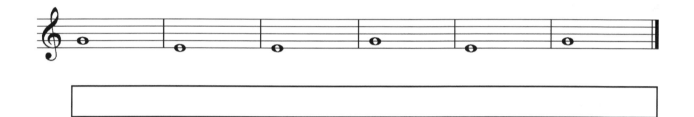

Write the names of the notes. Use colours: C-**yellow**, D-**green**, E-**blue**, F-**orange** and G-**red.**

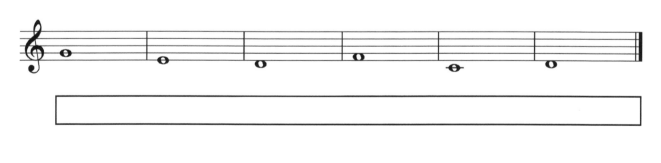

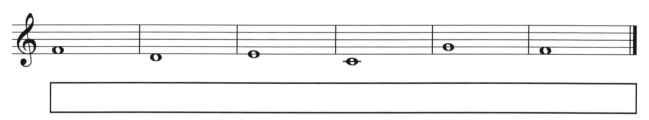

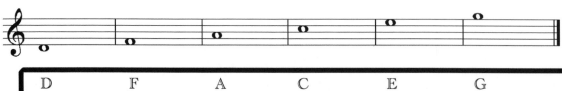

| D | F | A | C | E | G |

Help the penguin. Write the names of the notes on the <u>spaces</u>.

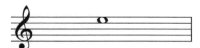

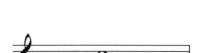

Clue

The note G is on the second line.

The notes on the lines

C   E   G   B   D   F

Help the penguin. Write the names of the notes on the <u>lines</u>.

Clue

The note G is on the second line.

## The Treble Clef

Match the notes with their names.

| Note | Name |
| --- | --- |
| | B |
| | C |
| | E |
| | A |
| | F |

16

Write the names of the following notes in the treble clef.

Answer the following questions:

- What's the name of the note on the second line in the treble clef? _____

- What's the name of the note on the fifth line in the treble clef? _____

- What's the name of the note on the second space in the treble clef? _____

- What's the name of the note on the fourth line in the treble clef? _____

- What's the name of the note on the third space in the treble clef? _____

NOTES: _____

_____

_____

Play the interactive application about the bass clef. It's located in the folder that accompanies this book:

"The bass clef".

The Bass clef

## The Bass Clef

The Bass Clef tells you that the note F is on the fourth line.

**Note F**  Fourth Line

Complete this sentence:

The music staff has _____lines and_____spaces.

The names of the notes in the bass clef are different from the ones in the treble clef.

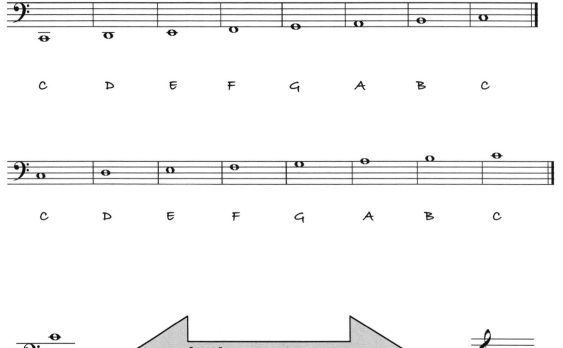

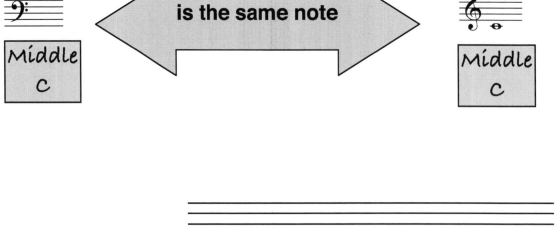

Use this staff to practice how to draw the bass clef. Remember to draw the two dots on the spaces around the fourth line.

? Draw the bass clef and the note **E**. Use a blue pencil.

Notes **E**, **F** and **G**.

Write the names of these notes.

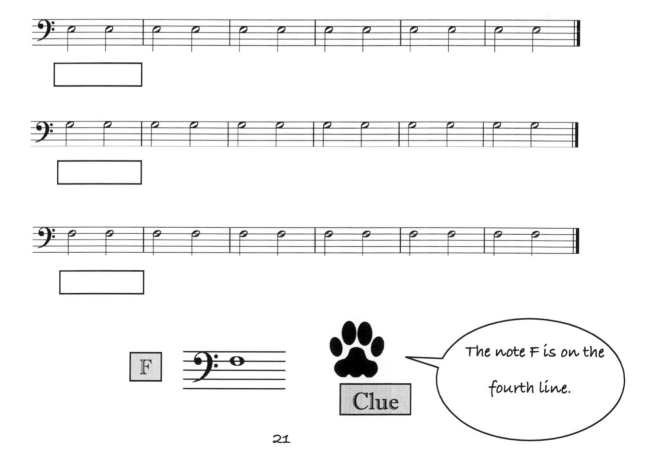

F

The note F is on the fourth line.

Clue

## The Bass Clef

**Notes from C to A.**

Draw the following notes in the bass clef.

| Notes | D | A | G | E | F | C |
|-------|---|---|---|---|---|---|

𝄢 𝄴

| Notes | E | F | G | D | A | C |
|-------|---|---|---|---|---|---|

𝄢 𝄴

## The notes on the spaces

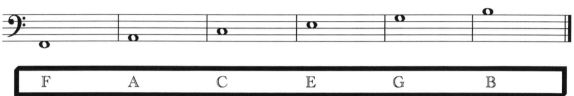

| F | A | C | E | G | B |

> Help the penguin. Write the names of the notes on the <u>spaces</u>.

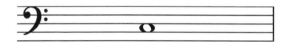

### Clue

The note F is on the fourth line.

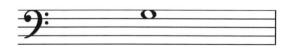

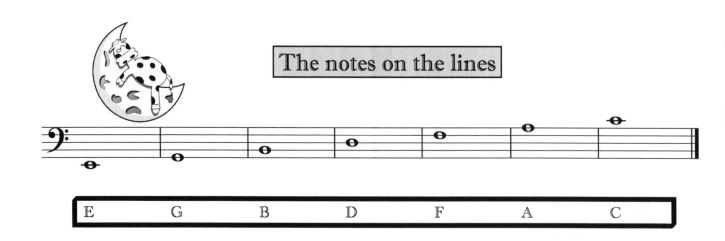

# The notes on the lines

| E | G | B | D | F | A | C |
|---|---|---|---|---|---|---|

Help the penguin. Write the names of the notes on the <u>lines</u>.

 Clue

The note F is on the fourth line.

## The Bass Clef

Match the notes with their names.

| Note | Name |
|---|---|
| | B |
| | C |
| | E |
| | A |
| | F |

C    D    E    F    G    A    B    C

Draw the bass clef and the note **D**.

F

Write the names of these notes.

# Good King Wenceslas

arr. Carla Louro

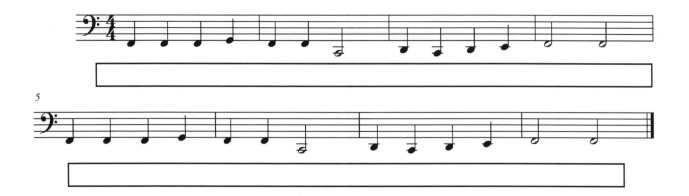

## Exercises about the bass clef

Write the names of the following notes in the bass clef.

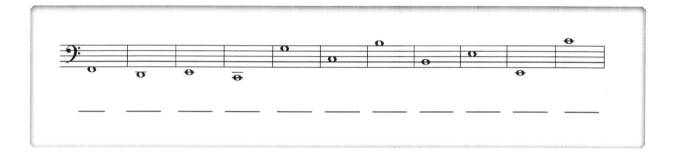

_____  _____  _____  _____  _____  _____  _____  _____  _____

Answer the following questions:

- What's the name of the note on the second line in the bass clef? _____

- What's the name of the note on the fifth line in the bass clef? _____

- What's the name of the note on the second space in the bass clef? _____

- What's the name of the note on the fourth line in the bass clef? _____

- What's the name of the note on the third space in the bass clef? _____

## Revision: read these notes.
## Treble clef.

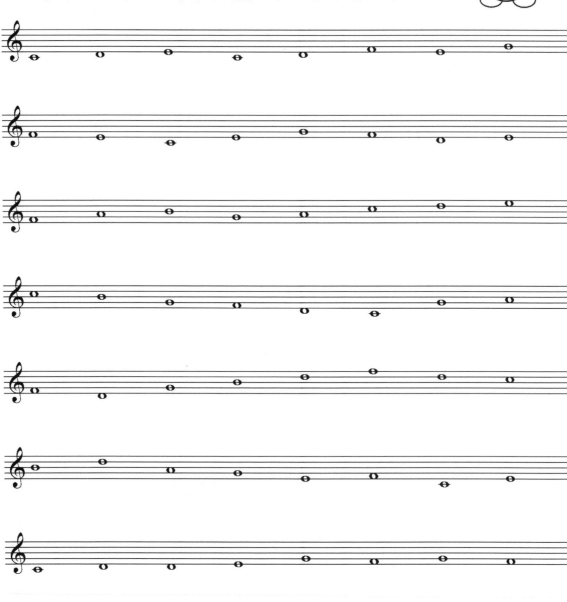

Read more notes in the treble clef. This exercise is more difficult than the exercise from the previous page.

**Revision: read these notes.**
**Bass clef.**

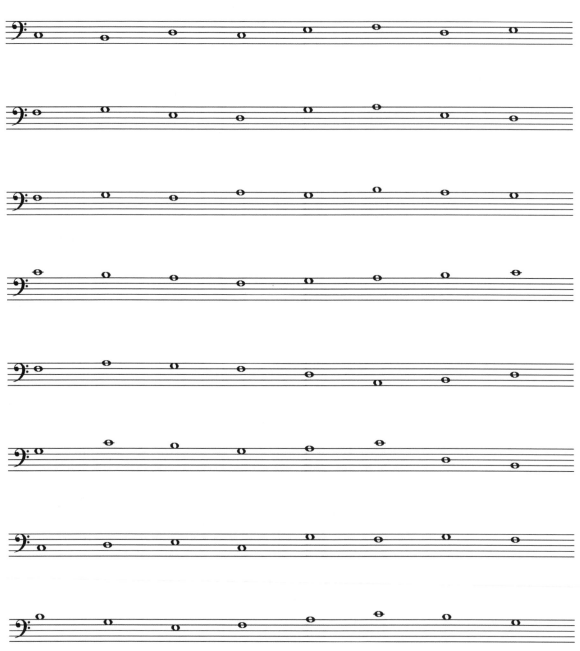

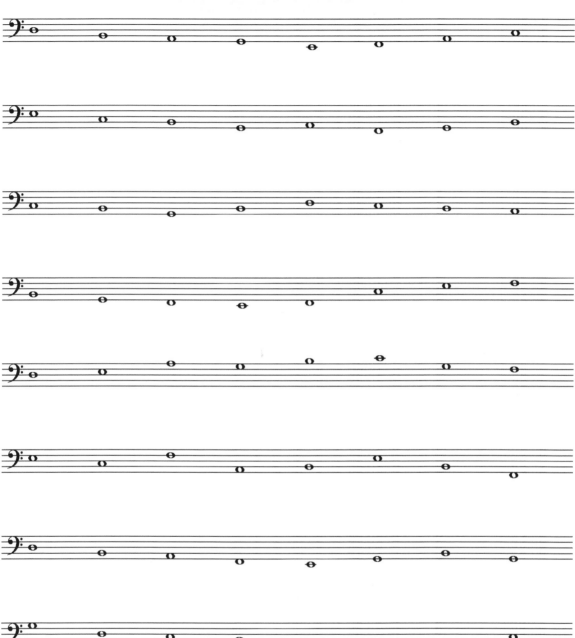

Read more notes on the bass clef. This exercise is more difficult than the exercise from the previous page.

NOTES: _____

_____

## WHAT DID YOU LEARN?

- ☐ What is the music staff?

- ☐ How to read notes on the treble clef?

- ☐ How to read notes on the bass clef?

- ☐ You completed the exercises about the musical notes.

## WHAT DO YOU STILL NEED TO PRACTICE?

Test dates:_____

Homework: _____

Concert dates: _____

Other: _____

### What do you still need to practice?

1. _____

2. _____

3. _____

NOTES: _____

_____

# 2
# Rhythm

The **Ant** will teach you everything about rhythm.

Crotchet

Minim

Chapter Two will teach you everything about rhythm.

You will learn what are semibreves, minims, crotchets and more.

You will learn theory about measures and barlines.

You will read and listen to rhythm.

You will practice **rhythm.**

*Good Work*

## Measures and Barlines

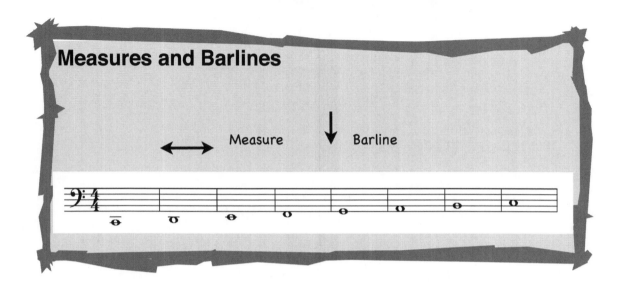

Measure          Barline

## Focus on Rhythm

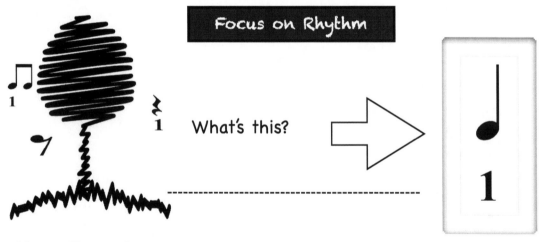

What's this?

1

## Note Duration

We speak of Note duration when we want to know how long we should play a note.

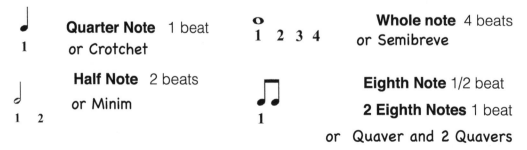

**Quarter Note** 1 beat
or Crotchet

**Half Note** 2 beats
or Minim

**Whole note** 4 beats
or Semibreve

**Eighth Note** 1/2 beat
**2 Eighth Notes** 1 beat
or Quaver and 2 Quavers

## Minims and Semibreves

**Minim** or **half note.**

2 beats.

The mp3 files with these rhythms and a metronome are located in a folder with the name of this book at www.arts2science.com.

**Semibreve** or **whole note.**

4 beats.

What did you learn?

Read these rhythms. Listen to tracks 1, 2, 3 and 4.

## Five note exercise
## Minims and Semibreves

The mp3 files with these rhythms and a metronome are located in a folder with the name of this book at www.arts2science.com.

Listen to track number 5.

- Read these notes. Be careful with their rhythm.

- You will play minims and semibreves.

**Rhythm and Notes Study**

**5**

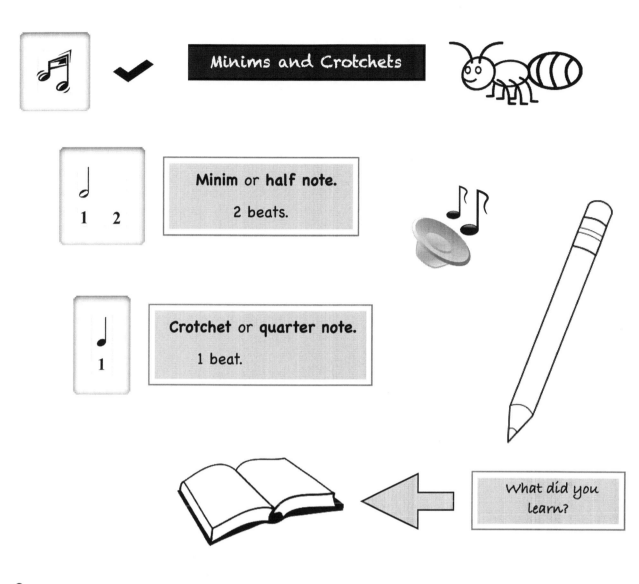

**Minims and Crotchets**

Minim or half note.

2 beats.

Crotchet or quarter note.

1 beat.

What did you learn?

**6**

Read these rhythms. Listen to tracks 6 and 7.

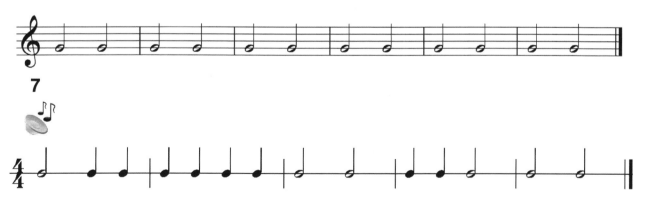

**7**

- Read these notes. Be careful with their rhythm.

- You will play minims and crotchets.

Listen to track number 8.

# Good King Wenceslas

arr. Carla Louro

**8**

"Good King Wenceslas" is a popular Christmas carol. This song tells the story of King Wenceslas, when he gave alms to a poor peasant on the Feast of Stephen (26th December), facing the cold winter weather.

## Quavers (eighth notes) exercises

2 quavers (eighth notes): 1 beat.

One quaver (eighth note): half beat.

**9**    Read the following rhythms. Listen to tracks 9, 10 and 11.

Place each number in the right box.

| Rhythm | Number |
|---|---|
| Crotchet, or quarter note. | |
| Semibreve, or whole note. | |

| Rhythm | Number |
|---|---|
| Minim, or half note. | |
| Two quavers, or two eighth notes. | |

1

**1**

1  2

**2**

1

**3**

o
1   2   3   4

**4**

Semiquavers and dotted minim

**semiquaver** or **sixteenth note.**

4 semiquavers: 1 beat.

**dotted minim** or **dotted half note.**

3 beats.

Attaching a dot to a note will add half of its value to its total duration.

Rhythm Exercises

**12**  Read the following rhythms. Listen to tracks 12 and 13.

**13**

43

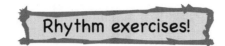
Rhythm exercises!

Draw:

| one | four | two | one | two | one |
|---|---|---|---|---|---|
| semibreve | crotchets | minims | semibreve | minims | semibreve |
| (whole note) | (quarter notes) | (half notes) | (whole note) | (half notes) | (whole note) |

How many crotchets (quarter notes) are there in the next example? --------------------

And how many minims (half notes)? ----------------------

How many crotchets (quarter notes) are there in the next example? --------------------

And how many quavers (eighth notes)? ----------------------

**Exercises about crotchet rests
(quarter note rests)**

**Crotchet rest (quarter note rest):**

1 beat (of silence).

The mp3 files with these rhythms
and a metronome are located in a
folder with the name of this book at
www.arts2science.com.

Read the following rhythms. Listen to tracks 14, 15 and 16.

## Rhythm

Match the rhythms with their names.

RHYTHM

| Rhythm | Name |
|---|---|
| 𝅝 **1**  2  3  4 | Crotchet or quarter note |
| 𝅗𝅥. **1**  2  3 | Semibreve or whole note |
| 𝅗𝅥 **1**  2 | Quavers or eighth notes |
| 𝅘𝅥 **1** | Minim or half note |
| 𝅘𝅥𝅮𝅘𝅥𝅮 **1** | Dotted minim or dotted half note |

 Rests and eighth note triplets

---

**Minim rest,** or **half note rest**: 2 beats of silence.

 The minim rest (half note rest) looks like a hat.

The **semibreve rest** (whole note rest) looks like an upside down hat.

---

**Quaver,** or **eighth note rest**: 1/2 beat of silence.

---

**Rests**     Rests are symbols that show how much time of silence is in the music. Each symbol shows the length of the rest.

| | | |
|---|---|---|
| Whole note rest<br>4 beats | Quarter note rest<br>1 beat | Sixteenth note rest<br>1/4 beat |
| Half note rest<br>2 beats | Eighth note rest<br>1/2 beat | Eighth note triplets<br>1 beat |

**Triplets**     Eighth note triplets are 3 eighth notes that are to be played in one beat, instead of the normal 2 eighth notes in one beat.

 **Rests**

WHAT'S THIS?   ⇨

   ----------------------------------

----------------------------------

47

# REVISION: BASS CLEF AND RHYTHM

Read this rhythm.

Rhythm!

Read this rhythm.

**The Bass Clef.**

Draw the following notes as semibreves in the bass clef:

G        E        D        C        F        A

E        D        G        C        F        B

Now you will see the notes on the staff. Write their names.

Note name:     A     C     _     _     _     _     _     _     _     _     _

_     _     _     _     _     _     _     _     _     _

## What's this?

_____

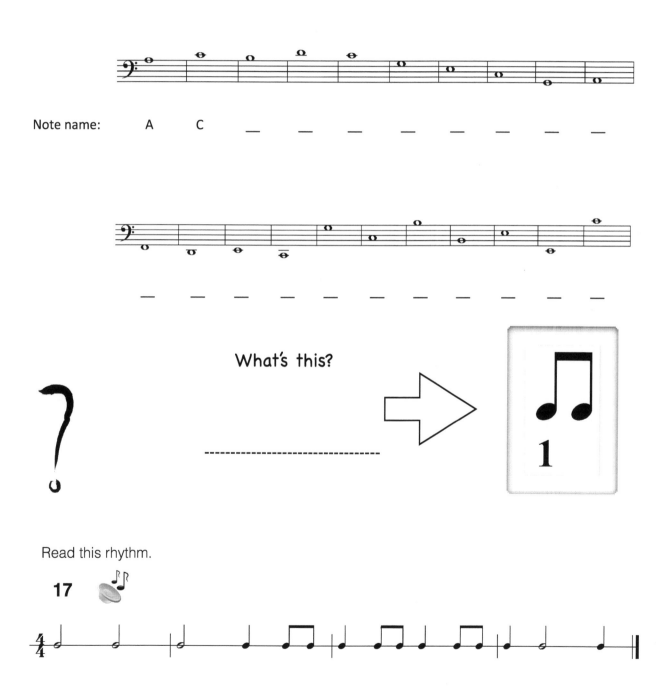

Read this rhythm.

**17**

**Exercises about rests**

Match the rests with their names.

 The minim rest looks like a hat.

Clue

| Rest | Name |
|---|---|
| ▬ | Quarter note (crotchet) rest |
| 𝄼 1 | Whole note (semibreve) rest |
| 𝄾 | Quaver rest (eighth note) rest |
| 𝄿 | Minim rest (half note) rest |
| ▬ | Semiquaver rest (sixteenth note) rest |

### Time Signature

The <u>time signature</u> tells you how long each measure is. There are several types of time signatures.

In <u>simple time</u> you have:

| **Duple Time** | **Triple Time** | **Quadruple Time** |
|---|---|---|
| Two quarter note beats in a bar | Three quarter note beats in a bar | Four quarter note beats in a bar |
| 2 | 3 | 4 |
| 4 | 4 | 4 |

## Write the time signature in each box. Read these rhythms.

Write the time signature in each box. Read the notes and rhythm of these melodies.

## Frère Jacques

Traditional french
arr. Carla Louro

## Swan Lake

Peter Ilych Tchaikovsky
arr. Carla Louro

Rhythm exercises.

The mp3 files with these rhythms
and a metronome are located in a
folder with the name of this book at
www.arts2science.com.

Read the following rhythms. Listen to tracks 18 to 22.

**dotted minim** or **dotted half note.**

3 beats.

1  2  3

Dotted quarter note, or
dotted crotchet.

1  2

Play a dotted quarter note,
followed by an eighth note.

Attaching a dot to a note will add
half of its value to its total duration.

Practice drawing a dotted
quarter note (dotted
crotchet), followed by an
eighth note (quaver).

------------------------------

------------------------------

The mp3 files with these rhythms and a metronome are located in a folder with the name of this book at www.arts2science.com.

Read the following rhythm. Listen to track 23.

**23**

Choose the right option to complete each measure.

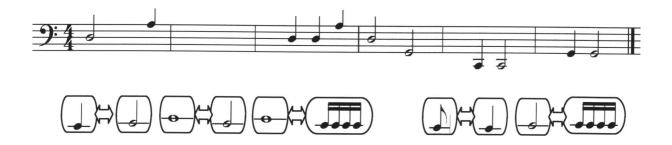

## WHAT DID YOU LEARN?

- [ ] Rhythm: crotchets, minims, semibreves and more.

- [ ] Barlines and time signatures in simple time.

- [ ] Hear and read rhythm.

- [ ] Rests.

## WHAT DO YOU STILL NEED TO PRACTICE?

Test dates:_____

Homework: _____

Concert dates: _____

Other: _____

### What do you still need to practice?

1. _____

2. _____

3. _____

NOTES: _____

_____

# 3

# Other elements of music

### Scales, dynamics, tempo marks, musical instruments and symbols.

The **Owl** will teach you several musical terms and abbreviations. You will learn about dynamics, sharps, flats and more.

Adagio
mf
Scales

Chapter Three will teach you several musical terms and abbreviations.

You will learn what are **dynamics** and **tempo marks.**

You will learn what are **key signatures** and **scales.**

You will see and hear music from several **composers.**

You will know musical instruments.

Scales

**Scales**   What is a **Scale**? A Scale is a sequence of notes that appear on ascending or descending order. A Major Scale has two half steps (semitones): the first between the third and the fourth degree of the scale and the second between the seventh and the eighth degree of the scale. The other intervals are whole steps (tones). An interval is the distance between two notes.

The diatonic scales have 7 different notes (degrees) and repeat the first one.

Look at the notes from the C Major scale, how they are ordered and how they are written:

Ascending C major Scale

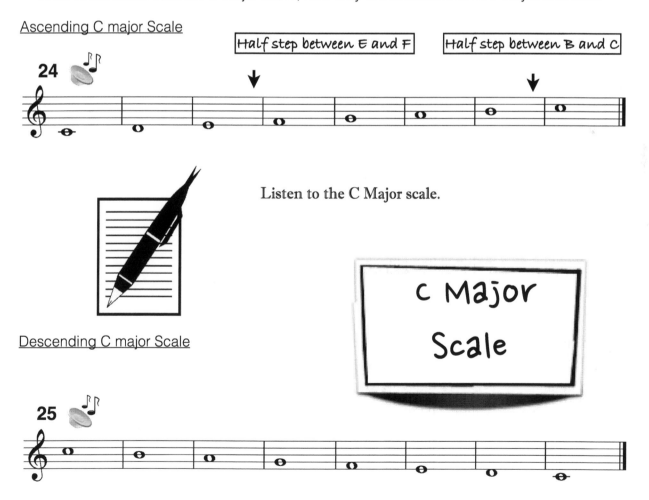

**Listen to the C Major scale.**

C Major Scale

Descending C major Scale

**Play the C Major Scale**

with the virtual piano

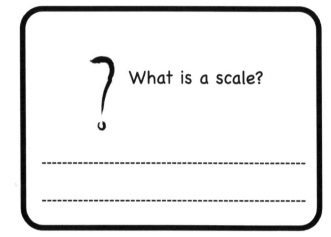

? What is a scale?

------------------------------------------------------------

------------------------------------------------------------

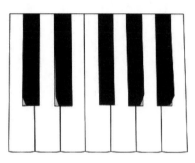

Where are the whole steps (tones) and the half steps (semitones)?

Notice the half steps (semitones) on a piano keyboard and in C Major.

Whole step from C to D

Whole step from D to E

Half step from E to F

Whole step from F to G

Whole step from G to A

Whole step from A to B

Half step from B to C

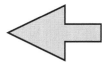 What did you learn?

Where are the half steps (semitones) in the C Major Scale? _____

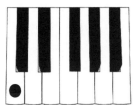 **Answer:**

# REVISION: THE BASS CLEF AND RHYTHM

Draw the notes from the C Major scale and then write down the note names. Write **whole step** or **half step** in the boxes.

Write down the names of the following notes in the Bass Clef.

SHARP

### Key Signature

The key signature appears in the beginning of the score, after the clef. It tells you which notes will be sharp or flat throughout the piece.

**Flat**

Sharp

The Sharp before the note means that you have to raise the note's pitch (a half step).

Flat

The Flat before the note means that you have to lower the note's pitch (a half step).

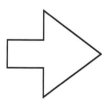

This symbol tells you that all the F notes, in any octave, are sharp throughout the piece, unless a natural symbol appears before the note F.

**Focus on Music Theory**

You play the G Major scale with an F sharp.

# G Major Scale

Listen to the G Major Scale.

**26**

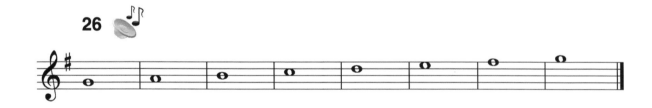

## Exercises about the G Major Scale

Write the names of the notes
from the G Major scale.

**Notes in G Major.**

Which note is sharp in
G Major?

---------------------------------

**Note name:**     G     A     ____  ____  ____  ____  ____

## Dynamics

We speak of *dynamics* when we want to express how loud or soft a sound is. There are several symbols to express this:

*p*    piano is an italian word for a soft sound.

*mp*   mezzo piano is louder than p.

*mf*   mezzo forte is louder than mp.

*f*    forte is an italian word for a loud sound.

BEETHOVEN

Listen to "Ode to Joy". This piece was written by **Beethoven**, a German composer and pianist from the **Classical Era** (1770-1827). This Composer made the transition between the Classical Era and Romantic Era.

## Ode to Joy

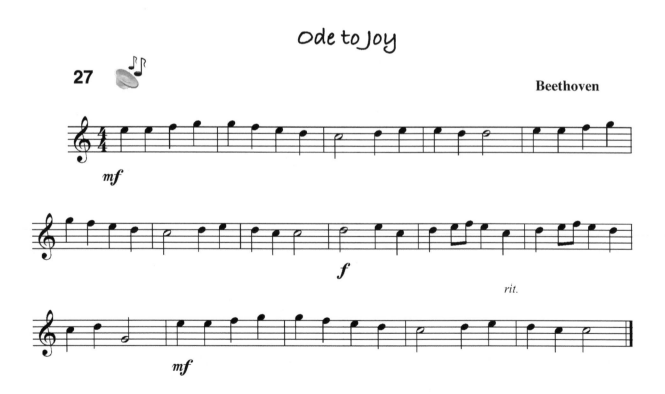

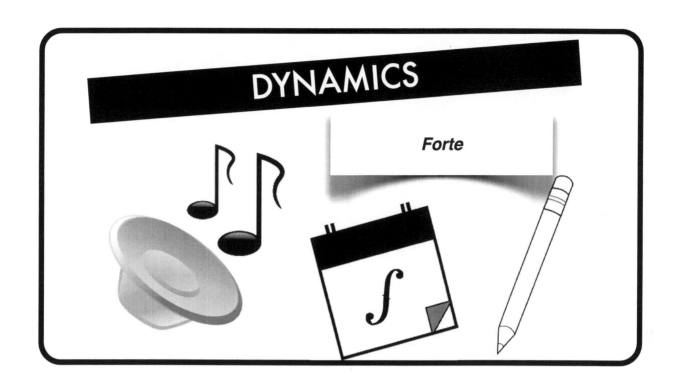

# DYNAMICS

**Forte**

Homework

What's the difference between *f* and *mp*?

------------------------------------

------------------------------------

## mf

Mezzo forte is louder than mp.

It describes the dynamics of a piece.

mf

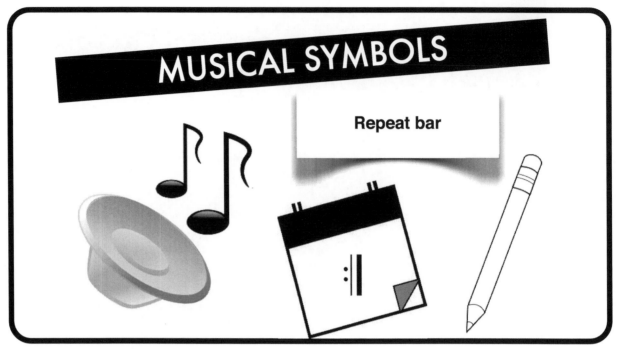

# MUSICAL SYMBOLS

**Repeat bar**

Homework

What's the difference between the repeat bar and the final barline?

-------------------------------

-------------------------------

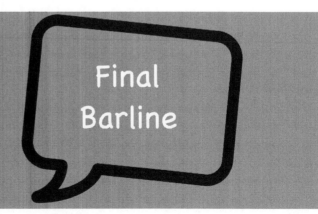

**Final Barline**

A final barline is a double barline in which the second bar is bold. You will see it at the end of a song.

Final Barline

| | | |
|---|---|---|
| **Natural Symbol** | ♮ | The Natural symbol cancels the previous accidentals of a note, which are created by the sharp and the flat symbols. |
| **Repeat Bar** | :‖ | The backward repeat bar tells you that you have to go back to the beginning of the piece or to the previous forward repeat bar. When the numbers **1.** and **2.** appear on top of the measure with the repeat symbol, you play the measure with **1.** the first time and the measure with **2.** the second time, not playing **1.**<br><br>Look at page 82 for a musical example. |

Where is the repeat bar in the next song?

_____

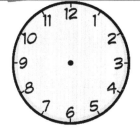

**28**  **Happy Birthday**

**Tie**    A <u>Tie</u> is a curved line that connects two notes that have the same pitch. It means that you should play them as a single note, with a duration that is the sum of the two notes. Note that the <u>Tie</u> is very similar to the <u>Slur</u>.

**Slur**    When you see the <u>Slur</u> between the notes, you play the notes without breaking the sound between them. The opposite of slurred is staccato.

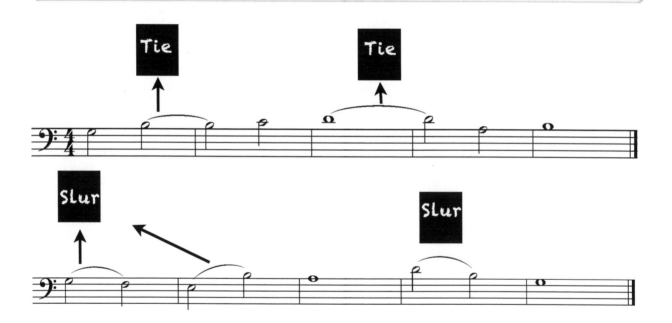

Staccato

When you play Staccato, you play short, detached notes. Staccato is represented by a dot above or below the note.

Match the musical symbols with their names.

| Musical Symbol | Name |
| --- | --- |
|  | Repeat bar |
| | Treble clef |
| # | Staccato |
| ♭ | Natural symbol |
| 𝄞 | Flat |
|  | Sharp |

Place each number in the right box.

| Symbol | Number |
|---|---|
| Sharp | |
| Staccato | |

| Symbol | Number |
|---|---|
| Natural | |
| Bass Clef | |

**1**

**2**

**3**

**4**

## Tempo Markings

Tempo is the speed of a piece.

Tempo markings are italian words that express the tempo (speed) of a piece. They tell us that the piece is slow or fast.

Lento — The music is slow.

Largo, Adagio — The same as Lento. The music is slow.

Andante, Moderato — The music isn't slow or fast.

Allegro — The music is fast.

Presto — The music is very fast.

# Musical examples: dynamics, tempo markings and composers.

## Frère Jacques

**29**

Traditional french
arr. Carla Louro

**Moderato** ♩ = 108

# DVORÀK

## New World Symphony

**30**

Adagio ♩ = 60

Dvoràk
arr. Carla Louro

## In the bleak mid-winter

**31**

Christmas carol
arr. Carla Louro

Andante ♩ = 80

# CHARPENTIER

Listen to this piece. It was written by **Marc-Antoine Charpentier**, a french composer from the **Baroque Era** (1643–1704).

## Te Deum

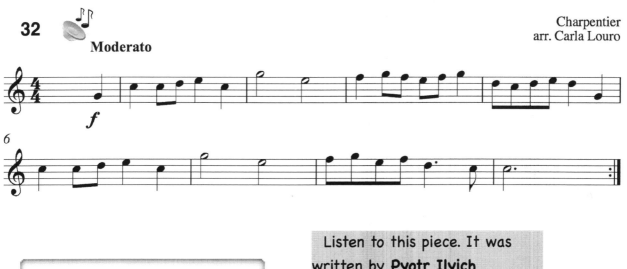

# TCHAIKOVSKY

Listen to this piece. It was written by **Pyotr Ilyich Tchaikovsky**, a russian composer from the **Romantic Era** (1840–1893).

## Swan Lake

# MUSICAL INSTRUMENTS

## Flute   VIOLIN

### String instruments

**Bowed Strings**
- Violin
- Viola
- Cello
- Double bass

**Plucked Strings**
- Guitar
- Harp
- Lute

### Wind instruments

**Brass instruments**
- Horn
- Trumpet
- Trombone
- Tuba

**Woodwind instruments**
- Flute
- Oboe
- Clarinet
- Saxophone
- Bassoon

<u>Keyboards</u>
- Piano
- Harpsichord
- Organ

<u>Percussion Instruments</u>
- Triangle
- Snare drum
- Marimba
- Timpani

# Match the instrument with the right phrase.

It's a bowed string instrument.

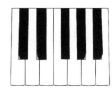 

It's a keyboard instrument.

It's a wind instrument.

It's a cello.

∫

Match the instruments with their names.

| Instrument | Name |
| --- | --- |

Flute

Violin

Percussion

Cello

Bassoon

## Musical instruments

Place each number in the right box.

| Instrument | Number | | Instrument | Number |
|---|---|---|---|---|
| Flute | | | Violin | |
| Bassoon | | | Cello | |

**1**

**2**

**3**

**4**

Learn more about musical instruments. Open the app "Introduction to the orchestra". You can find it in the folder that accompanies this book.

# <u>REVISION</u>: THE TREBLE CLEF, THE BASS CLEF, RHYTHM, SYMBOLS AND INSTRUMENTS.

## Complete the phrases. Choose the right option.

- The violin is a (string/wind)_____instrument.

- The guitar is a (plucked/bowed)_____string instrument.

- The trumpet is a (brass/woodwind)_____instrument.

- The minim (half note) is worth (3/2)_____beats.

- The semibreve (whole note) is worth (4/2)_____beats.

- Attaching a dot to a note will add (one beat/half of its value)_____ to its total duration.

- Adagio means that we will play the piece (fast/slowly)_____.

- *p* is related to (dynamics/tempo)_____.

- The symbol :‖ is called (sharp/repeat bar)_____.

- Beethoven was a composer from the (Baroque/Classical)_____Era.

## Musical Symbols

Draw each symbol in the right box.

| | | |
|---|---|---|
| Forte | Piano | Crescendo |

| | | |
|---|---|---|
| Fermata | Decrescendo | Natural Symbol |

| | | |
|---|---|---|
| The Bass Clef | The Treble Clef | Sharp Symbol |

𝒇   𝒑   𝄢   ⌢   >   ♯ 𝄞   <   ♮

## CHRISTMAS SONG IN D MAJOR

### The First Noel

Christmas carol
arr. Carla Louro

**34**

---

## Lyrics

The First Noel, the Angels did say
was to certain poor shepherds in fields as
they lay.
In fields where they lay keeping their sheep
On a cold winter's night that was so deep.
Noel, Noel, Noel, Noel
Born is the King of Israel!

## ABOUT THE PREVIOUS PIECE

### Answer the following questions about the previous piece:

1 - The music is written in which clef? ------------------

2 - Which notes are sharp?

-----------------------------------------------------------------

3 - Locate the **repeat bar**.

4 - Locate the symbol "crescendo".

5 - What do these terms and abbreviations mean?

*Moderato:* -------------------------------------------------------------------------

*mp:* -------------------------------------------------------------------------

*1. and 2.:* -------------------------------------------------------------------------

# C Major

**35**

## New World Symphony

Largo

Dvoràk
arr. Carla Louro

## ABOUT THE PREVIOUS PIECE

### Answer the following questions about the previous piece:

1 - Locate the symbol "decrescendo". ----------------------------------

2 - A dotted crotchet (dotted quarter note) is worth ------------ beats.

3 - Locate the **final barline**.

4 - What does Largo mean? -------------------------------------------

5 - What do these terms and abbreviations mean?

*rit.:* ----------------------------------------------------------------

*mf:* -----------------------------------------------------------------

6 - How many measures are there in the piece?

----------------------------------------------------------------

## WHAT DID YOU LEARN?

✔

- ☐ What are dynamics and tempo marks?

- ☐ What are key signatures and scales?

- ☐ Music from several composers.

- ☐ Musical instruments.

## WHAT DO YOU STILL NEED TO PRACTICE?

Test dates:_____

Homework: _____

Concert dates: _____

Other: _____

## What do you still need to practice?

1. _____

2. _____

3. _____

# Revision exercises: clefs and rhythm

Notes: draw the notes on the music staff.
You will write them in the treble clef and in the bass clef.

F    A    D    C    E    B    E    D    G    D    C

G    E    A    D    A    F    E    C    G    C    F

F    E    A    C    A    B    G    F    G    D    C

F    E    D    F    A    G    E    C    F    D    E

**Rhythm dictations: write the rhythms that you hear. Listen to tracks 36 and 37.**

36

37

Notes: draw the notes on the music staff.
You will write them in the treble clef and in the bass clef.

F    E    C    G    A    D    E    C    F    D    C

A    B    D    C    F    B    D    F    G    E    A

B    E    D    F    A    F    E    C    G    D    A

F    B    A    C    A    B    G    C    A    F    C

**Rhythm dictations: write the rhythms that you hear. Listen to tracks 38 and 39.**

38

39

# Revision exercises: clefs and rhythm

Notes: draw the notes on the music staff.
You will write them in the treble clef and in the bass clef.

𝄞

G  E  B  C  A  D  E  C  G  E  C

𝄞

F  A  D  E  A  B  G  D  G  D  C

𝄞

F  E  D  C  G  B  E  F  G  D  C

𝄢

A  B  C  G  A  F  E  C  G  B  C

**Rhythm dictations: write the rhythms that you hear. Listen to tracks 40 and 41.**

40 ‖

41 ‖

# Revision exercises: clefs and rhythm

Notes: draw the notes on the music staff.
You will write them in the treble clef and in the bass clef.

F    D    G    C    E    B    F    C    A    D    E

D    E    F    G    A    B    F    C    G    E    C

G    E    D    F    A    G    E    D    F    D    C

F    E    D    C    A    B    E    C    G    D    C

**Rhythm dictations: write the rhythms that you hear. Listen to tracks 42 and 43.**

42

43

90

Solutions: rhythm dictations. Read the following rhythms.

**36**

**37**

**38** 4/4

**39** 2/4

**40** 4/4

**41** 2/4

**42** 3/4

**43** 4/4

Play the piece loudly.

Lower a semitone (half step).

It's a wind instrument.

It's the repeat bar.

NOTES: _____

_____

NOTES: _____

_____

NOTES: _____

_____

# FLASHCARDS: NOTES IN THE TREBLE CLEF.

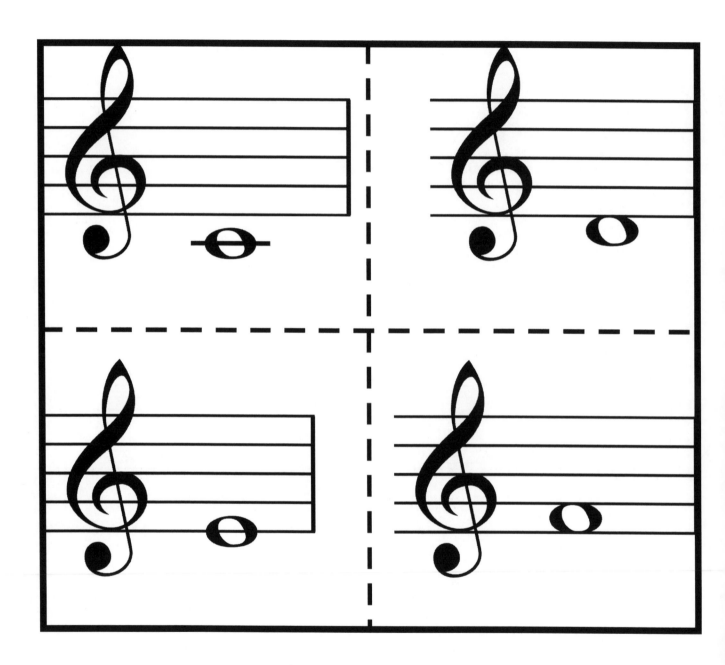

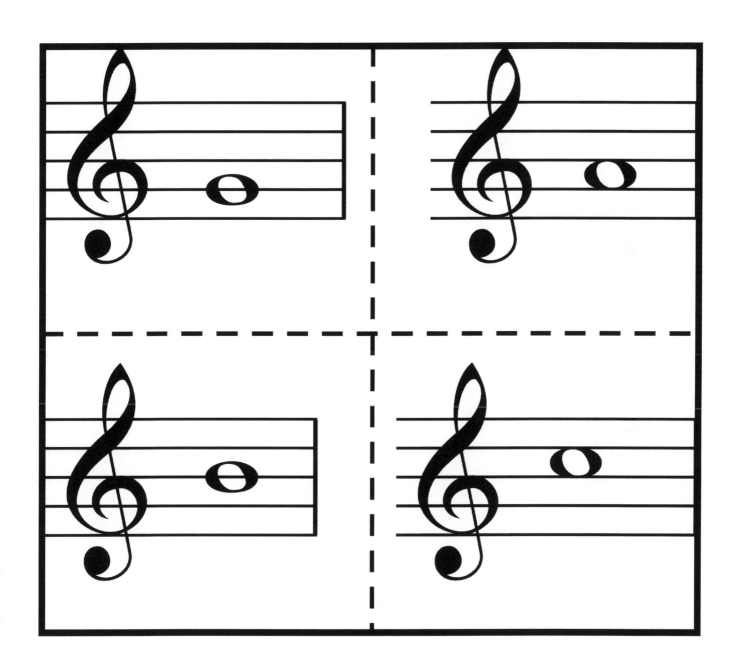

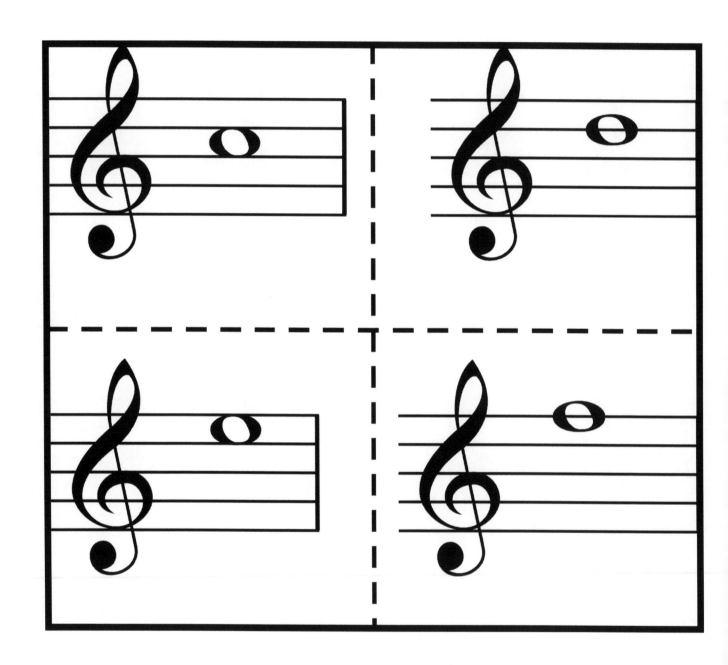

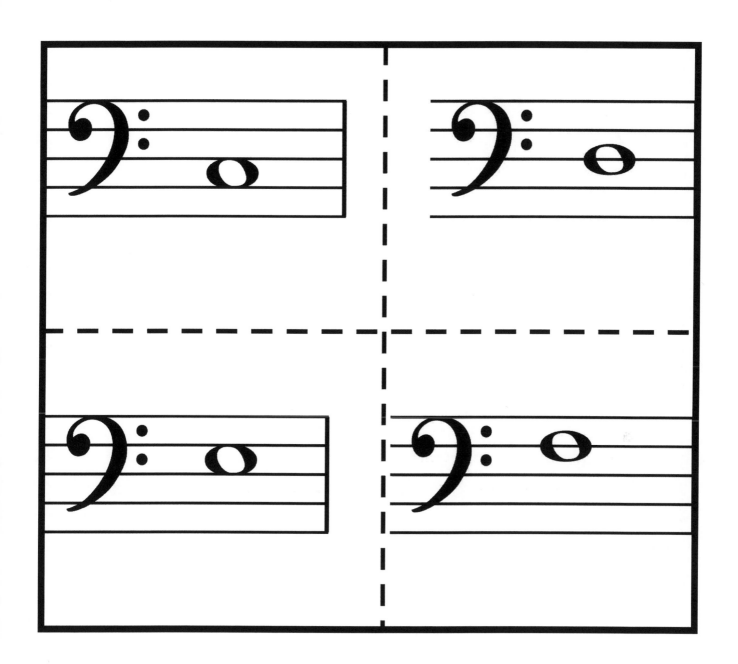

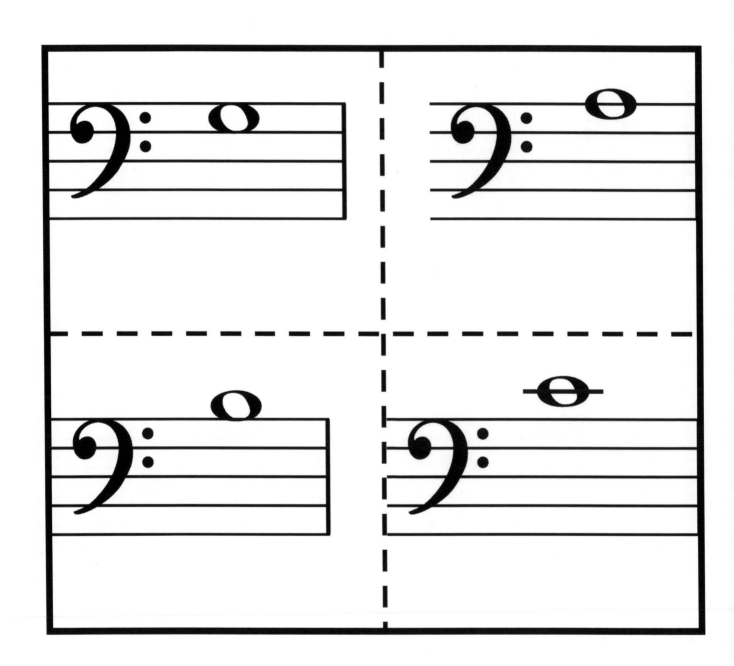

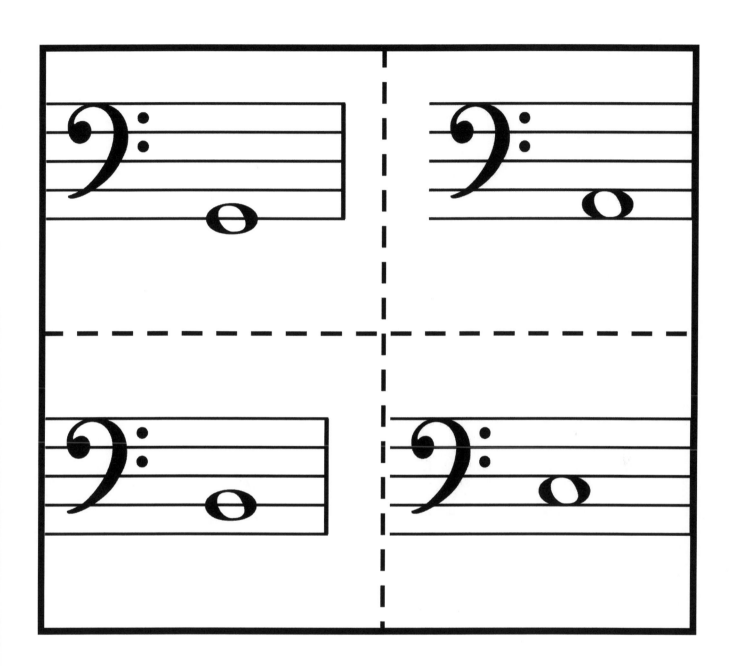

# FLASHCARDS: RHYTHM.

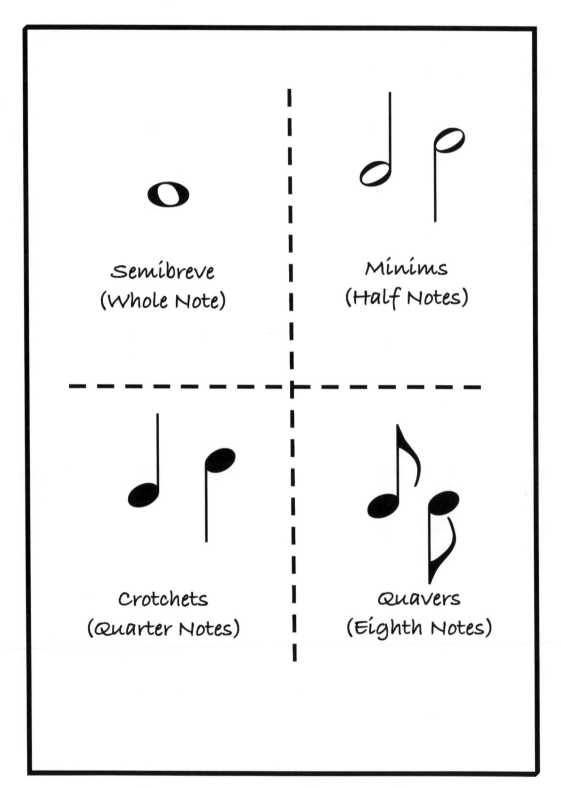

Semibreve
(Whole Note)

Minims
(Half Notes)

Crotchets
(Quarter Notes)

Quavers
(Eighth Notes)

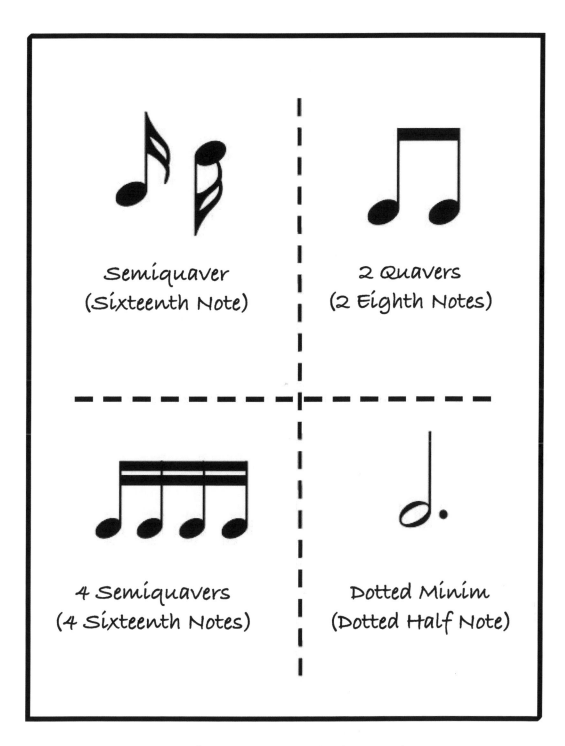

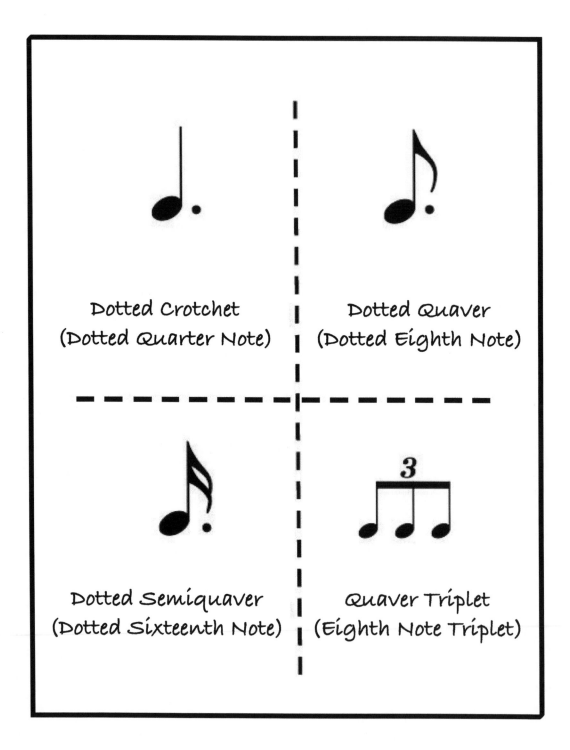

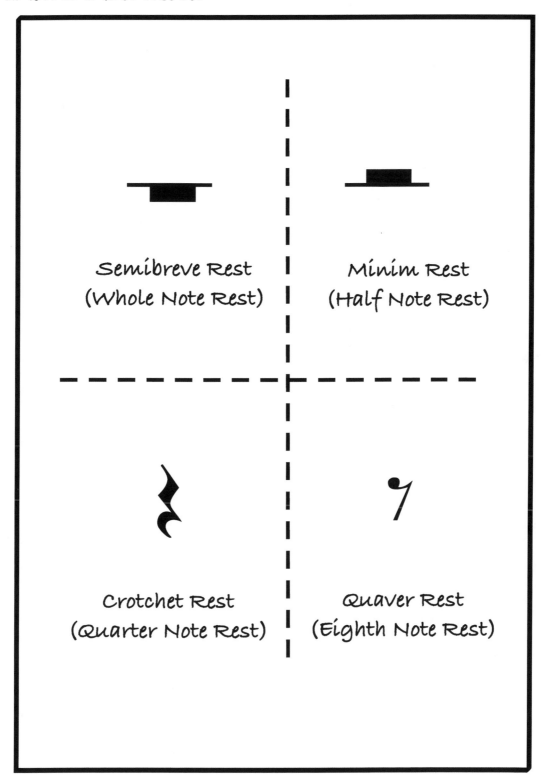

Semibreve Rest
(Whole Note Rest)

Minim Rest
(Half Note Rest)

Crotchet Rest
(Quarter Note Rest)

Quaver Rest
(Eighth Note Rest)

*Use this page to plan your year. Take notes of important dates and of your homework.*

**Student's Notes**

------------------------------------------------

------------------------------------------------

------------------------------------------------

------------------------------------------------

------------------------------------------------

Test dates:_____

Homework: _____

Concert Dates: _____

Other: _____

| Date | Homework | Page |
|---|---|---|
|  |  |  |
|  |  |  |
|  |  |  |
|  |  |  |
|  |  |  |
|  |  |  |
|  |  |  |
|  |  |  |
|  |  |  |
|  |  |  |
|  |  |  |
|  |  |  |
|  |  |  |
|  |  |  |
|  |  |  |
|  |  |  |
|  |  |  |
|  |  |  |
|  |  |  |
|  |  |  |
|  |  |  |
|  |  |  |
|  |  |  |
|  |  |  |

Printed in Great Britain
by Amazon.co.uk, Ltd.,
Marston Gate.